Congressional
Research Service
Informing the legislative debate since 1914 _____

U.S. Foreign Aid to the Palestinians

Jim Zanotti
Specialist in Middle Eastern Affairs

July 3, 2014

Congressional Research Service

7-5700

www.crs.gov

RS22967

Summary

Since the establishment of limited Palestinian self-rule in the West Bank and Gaza Strip in the mid-1990s, the U.S. government has committed approximately $5 billion in bilateral assistance to the Palestinians, who are among the world's largest per capita recipients of international foreign aid. Successive Administrations have requested aid for the Palestinians in apparent support of at least three major U.S. policy priorities of interest to Congress:

- Preventing terrorism against Israel from Hamas and other militant organizations.

- Fostering stability, prosperity, and self-governance in the West Bank that inclines Palestinians toward peaceful coexistence with Israel and a "two-state solution."

- Meeting humanitarian needs.

Between June 2007 and June 2014, these U.S. policy priorities crystallized around the factional and geographical split between the Fatah-led Palestinian Authority (PA) in the West Bank and Hamas in the Gaza Strip. The formation of a PA government in June 2014 pursuant to a Fatah-Hamas agreement has raised a number of questions regarding the implications for Palestinian unity, prospects for Israeli-Palestinian peace and security, and U.S. aid. The Obama Administration has stated its intent to continue financial assistance to the PA and to carefully monitor the new government's composition and actions, while several Members of Congress have voiced skepticism and are considering changing conditions under which aid can flow to the PA.

From FY2008 to the present, annual Economic Support Fund (ESF) assistance to the West Bank and Gaza Strip has averaged around $400 million, with that amount divided between U.S. Agency for International Development (USAID)-administered project assistance (through grants to contracting organizations) and direct budgetary assistance to the Palestinian Authority (PA). Annual International Narcotics Control and Law Enforcement (INCLE) nonlethal assistance for PA security forces and the criminal justice sector in the West Bank has averaged around $100 million. In line with Obama Administration requests, funding levels declined slightly in FY2013, with a new baseline of overall annual ESF assistance of $370 million, and a new baseline of annual INCLE assistance of $70 million.

Because of congressional concerns that, among other things, U.S. aid to the Palestinians might be diverted to Palestinian terrorist groups, the aid is subject to a host of vetting and oversight requirements and legislative restrictions. Additionally, since FY2011, Congress has taken various forms of action in response to Palestinian initiatives in the United Nations and other international forums aimed at increasing international recognition of Palestinian statehood outside of negotiations with Israel. Additionally, the United States is the largest single-state donor to the U.N. Relief and Works Agency for Palestine Refugees in the Near East (UNRWA).

U.S. assistance to the Palestinians is given alongside assistance from other international donors, and U.S. policy makers routinely call for greater or more timely assistance from Arab governments in line with pledges those governments make. The PA remains dependent on external donor assistance to meet its budgetary needs—especially its large public payroll—and it also seeks foreign investment to jumpstart its private sector. Even if the immediate objectives of U.S. assistance programs for the Palestinians are met, the long-term utility of U.S. aid in encouraging regional stability and Palestinian economic and political self-sufficiency might depend to some extent on progress toward a political solution that addresses Palestinian national aspirations and Israeli security demands.

Contents

Figures

Tables

Appendixes

Contacts

Overview

Since the establishment of limited Palestinian self-rule in the West Bank and Gaza Strip in the mid-1990s, the U.S. government has committed more than $5 billion in bilateral assistance to the Palestinians in the West Bank and Gaza,[1] who are among the largest per capita recipients of foreign aid worldwide.[2] U.S. aid to the Palestinians is intended to promote at least three major U.S. policy priorities of interest to Congress:

- Preventing terrorism against Israel from the Sunni Islamist group Hamas[3] and other militant organizations.

- Fostering stability, prosperity, and self-governance that incline Palestinians toward peaceful coexistence with Israel and a "two-state solution."

- Meeting humanitarian needs.

For the seven years from June 2007 to June 2014, U.S. aid to the Palestinians occurred within the context of a geographical and factional split between

1. *West Bank/Fatah*: a U.S.- and Western-supported Palestinian Authority (PA) in the West Bank led by President Mahmoud Abbas (who also leads the secular nationalist Fatah faction and the Palestine Liberation Organization, or PLO)[4]; and

2. *Gaza Strip/Hamas*: a de facto regime led by Hamas in Gaza.

This split has been called into question by an April 2014 agreement between Fatah and Hamas that led to the June 2014 formation of a new "interim" or "caretaker" PA government with nominal sway over PA-controlled areas in both the West Bank and Gaza (see "What Does the Fatah-Hamas "Unity" Government Mean for U.S. Aid?" below).[5]

---

[1] Prior to the establishment of limited Palestinian self-rule in the West Bank and Gaza, approximately $170 million in U.S. developmental and humanitarian assistance (not including contributions to UNRWA) were obligated for Palestinians in the West Bank and Gaza from 1975-1993, mainly through nongovernmental organizations. CRS Report 93-689 F, *West Bank/Gaza Strip: U.S. Foreign Assistance*, by Clyde R. Mark, July 27, 1993, available on request to Jim Zanotti.

[2] Net official development assistance per capita figures for all countries for 2007-2011 are available at http://data.worldbank.org/indicator/DT.ODA.ODAT.PC.ZS.

[3] Hamas has been designated a Foreign Terrorist Organization (FTO), a Specially Designated Terrorist (SDT), and a Specially Designated Global Terrorist (SDGT) by the U.S. government.

[4] The PLO is the generally recognized international representative of the Palestinian people. The PA was created pursuant to various Israel-PLO agreements during the Oslo process in the 1990s as the organ of governance for limited Palestinian self-rule in the West Bank and Gaza Strip. Officially, the PLO represents the Palestinian national movement in international bodies, including the United Nations. However, some characterizations of Palestinian efforts in recent years to garner international support for statehood refer to the PA's involvement because Mahmoud Abbas leads both the PLO and the PA, because some other PA officials (including Foreign Minister Riad Malki) have been publicly involved in the efforts, and because one could argue that the territorial writ of the PA involves it in any issue pertaining to the possible establishment of a Palestinian state within provisional or permanent borders. For the remainder of this report, references to "PLO" initiatives in the United Nations regarding statehood will be construed as referring both to PLO and PA participation, to the extent it exists.

[5] For a list of the government's ministers, see "New members of unity govt named," *Ma'an News Agency*, June 3, 2014.

After the split took place in June 2007, the United States boosted aid levels to the Palestinians, with most assistance going in direct support of the PA's security, governance, development, and reform programs in the West Bank under Abbas (including during the 2007-2013 tenure of former PA prime minister Salam Fayyad), presumably in part to counter Hamas in Gaza. As a result, the post-2007 annual average of U.S. bilateral assistance is substantially greater than the approximate annual average of $170 million from 2000-2007 and $70 million from 1994-1999, years largely marked by the rule of the late Yasser Arafat, who died in late 2004.

From FY2008 to the present, annual Economic Support Fund (ESF) assistance to the West Bank and Gaza Strip has averaged around $400 million, with that amount divided between U.S. Agency for International Development (USAID)-administered project assistance (through grants to contracting organizations) and direct budgetary assistance to the Palestinian Authority (PA). Annual International Narcotics Control and Law Enforcement (INCLE) nonlethal assistance for PA security forces and the criminal justice sector in the West Bank has averaged around $100 million. In line with Obama Administration requests, funding levels declined slightly in FY2013, with a new baseline of overall annual ESF assistance of $370 million, and a new baseline of annual INCLE assistance of $70 million. Administration requests for ESF and INCLE have remained constant for FY2014 and FY2015. Some FY2013 ESF funding has been provided via the ESF-Overseas Contingency Operations (OCO) account, and the State Department expects to draw from this account in FY2014 as well.

Table 1. U.S. Bilateral Assistance to the Palestinians, FY2008-FY2015

(regular and supplemental appropriations; current year $ in millions)

Account	FY2008	FY2009	FY2010	FY2011	FY2012	FY2013	FY2014	FY2015
ESF	389.5	776.0	400.4	395.7	395.7	356.7	272.0	370.0
ESF-OCO	-	-	-	-	-	10.0	98.0	-
INCLE	25.0	184.0	100.0	150.0	100.0	70.0	70.0	70.0
Total	**414.5**	**960.0**	**500.4**	**545.7**	**495.7**	**437.2**	**440.0**	**441.0**

Sources: U.S. State Department, USAID.

Notes: All amounts are approximate. Amounts stated for FY2015 have been requested but not appropriated. For FY2015, the Obama Administration has requested an additional $1 million from the Nonproliferation, Anti-terrorism, Demining, and Related Programs (NADR) account.

Additional U.S. humanitarian assistance for Palestinian refugees in Gaza and elsewhere continues through contributions to the U.N. Relief and Works Agency for Palestine Refugees in the Near East (UNRWA). U.S. contributions to UNRWA, which have totaled more than $4.9 billion since UNRWA's inception in 1950 (see **Table 2** below), have averaged over $200 million annually since 2007.

The effectiveness of U.S. assistance to the Palestinians in furthering U.S. policy objectives is challenged, logistically and strategically, by the shifting and often conflicting interests of Israel and various Palestinian groups. Effectiveness is also challenged by the U.S. interagency process, as well as the need to coordinate activities and assistance with other donor states and with international organizations and coordinating mechanisms such as the European Union (EU),

United Nations,[6] World Bank, the Office of the Quartet Representative, and the Ad Hoc Liaison Committee,[7] among others.

What Does the Fatah-Hamas "Unity" Government Mean for U.S. Aid?

Recent Developments, Uncertainties, and FY2014 Aid

As mentioned above, in June 2014, Abbas swore in a new PA caretaker government with nominal authority over PA-controlled areas in both the West Bank and Gaza, in accordance with an April 2014 Fatah-Hamas agreement. At the same time, Hamas's de facto ministers in Gaza left their posts. The new government does not include any ministers from Hamas and has publicly stated commitments to nonviolent coexistence with Israel and to upholding formal obligations reflected in past Israeli-Palestinian agreements. In the aftermath of the alleged murder of three Israeli teenagers by two West Bank Palestinians with apparent Hamas ties, as of early July 2014, Israel was reportedly pressing Mahmoud Abbas to dissolve the Hamas-approved PA government. If Abbas elects to continue the government's tenure, the following questions appear to have relevance to the current situation:

- To what extent, if at all, can the new government practically consolidate control over Gaza, especially in relation to security enforcement, given the continued presence of militias controlled by Hamas and other armed groups?

- Can the PA find a financially and politically workable way to address the situation faced by 42,000 people in Gaza previously employed as civil servants by Hamas?[8]

- What is the likelihood that PA presidential and parliamentary elections contemplated in the April 2014 Fatah-Hamas agreement might take place, and could they lead to a permanent end to the Palestinians' geographical and factional split? If such elections do take place, what is their probable timing?

- As a result of the new government, to what extent, if at all, will the PA change its (1) approach to domestic political reform and economic development, (2) diplomatic approach to its disputes with Israel, and/or (3) the nature and extent of its West Bank security cooperation with Israel?

---

[6] Over the years, U.N. organs have set up a number of bodies or offices, as well as five U.N. peacekeeping operations, which have or had mandates or functions directly related to Palestine or the Arab-Israeli dispute.

[7] The Ad Hoc Liaison Committee is a coordinating mechanism for Israel, the PA, and all major international actors providing assistance to the Palestinians that was established in the mid-1990s to facilitate reform and development in the West Bank and Gaza in connection with the Oslo process. Norway permanently chairs the committee, which meets periodically in various international venues and is divided into sectors with their own heads for discrete issue areas such as economic development, security and justice, and civil society.

[8] Fares Akram and Jodi Rudoren, "Issue of Pay for 2 Sets of Workers Tugs at Palestinian Pact," *New York Times*, June 27, 2014. The PA already faces regular difficulties in meeting its various budgetary obligations, particularly salaries for its own approximately 150,000 employees.

The Obama Administration has stated its intent to continue financial assistance to the PA and to carefully monitor the new government's composition and actions.[9] Several Members of Congress have expressed skepticism about providing U.S. assistance to any PA government approved by Hamas, and some have proposed legislation that would change the conditions on aid to such a government (see "Conditions on Funding Hamas-Approved PA Government" below).[10]

To date, the only distribution of FY2014 aid to the Palestinians has been $15 million in ESF project assistance through contracting organizations.[11] Regarding possible future ESF distributions (for both project assistance and direct budgetary assistance to the PA) in FY2014, according to July 3, 2014, email correspondence from a State Department official to CRS, "Given the current political context, the Department of State is working closely with the interagency and with the Hill to determine the best way forward on notification. No final decisions have been made."

Regarding the possible effect of delays in distributing aid, a U.S. Agency for International Development (USAID) official made the following statement to CRS via email on June 23, 2014:

> Several USAID programs in education, health, infrastructure, and economic growth, which contribute to continued political and economic stability in the West Bank and Gaza and the viability of a two-state solution, are currently in urgent need of funding. If funding is not received, crucial development gains may be jeopardized.

For information on possible INCLE security assistance distributions in FY2014, see "U.S. Security Assistance to the Palestinian Authority" below.

Current and Past Legislative Conditions

Current conditions regarding a "power-sharing PA government" involving Hamas are as follows. No aid is permitted for a power-sharing PA government that includes Hamas as a member, or that results from an agreement with Hamas and over which Hamas exercises "undue influence," unless the President certifies that the PA government, including all ministers, has "publicly accepted and is complying with" the following two principles embodied in Section 620K of the Palestinian Anti-Terrorism Act of 2006 (PATA), P.L. 109-446: (1) recognition of "the Jewish state of Israel's right to exist" and (2) acceptance of previous Israeli-Palestinian agreements (the "Section 620K principles").[12] If the PA government is "Hamas-controlled," PATA applies additional conditions, limitations, and restrictions on aid. Under PATA, in the event that Hamas participation in a PA government precludes ministries from receiving aid, the PA President and judiciary (if not Hamas-controlled) may under certain conditions receive aid pursuant to a presidential waiver for national security purposes.

---

[9] State Department Daily Press Briefing, June 1, 2014.

[10] "U.S. lawmakers want to hold aid to new Palestinian unity government," *Reuters*, June 2, 2014.

[11] USAID FY2014 Congressional Notification #39, November 8, 2013. The notification also included $10 million in FY2013 ESF-OCO funding.

[12] Consolidated Appropriations Act, 2014 (P.L. 113-76), §7040(f). The Section 620K principles have some similarity to the principles the so-called international Quartet (United States, European Union, U.N. Secretary-General's office, and Russia) has required Hamas to meet before accepting dealings with it: (1) recognizing Israel's right to exist, (2) renouncing violence, and (3) accepting previous Israeli-Palestinian agreements.

It is unclear whether the PA government established in June 2014 is either subject to the "undue influence" of Hamas or "Hamas-controlled," thus potentially triggering the conditions on U.S. aid cited above. The Obama Administration does not appear to have made a determination that either undue influence or Hamas control applies in this case, though some Members of Congress have voiced concerns regarding the issue. Under PATA, the Palestinian Legislative Council (PLC) is considered to be part of the PA, but the legal consequences if the PLC were to reconvene with the majority Hamas won in 2006 are unclear.[13]

Conditions regarding U.S. aid to a power-sharing PA government were different in FY2008 and FY2009 appropriations legislation than they have been since FY2010. Under the previous conditions, in the event of a power-sharing PA government formed with Hamas as "a member," U.S. aid would have been prohibited unless Hamas (as opposed to the government and its ministers) had accepted the Section 620K principles.[14]

See "FY2015 Appropriations Process" below for legislative proposals and possible questions for Congress regarding this issue.

Other Issues for Congress

Questions regarding the advisability of aid and its effective implementation also exist with regard to other issues. Such issues include past and possible future initiatives—such as at the United Nations or the International Criminal Court (ICC)—aimed at bolstering international support for Palestinian statehood. In connection with these issues, informal congressional holds (see **Appendix A**) delayed significant portions of already-appropriated FY2011 and FY2012 U.S. aid. These holds were eventually released. Subsequently, Congress has enacted provisions that would restrict aid to the PA as a result of certain international initiatives (see discussion below). Public debate has intensified over the advisability and probability of future Palestinian international initiatives after the latest round of Israel-PLO negotiations ended in April 2014 without agreement on issues of dispute or a way forward. On April 1, Mahmoud Abbas signed documents aimed at having "Palestine" accede to 15 multilateral treaties and conventions.[15] Accession is proceeding in accordance with the specific provisions set forth in each treaty or convention.

---

[13] Although a Hamas-majority PLC could technically pass legislation controlling various functions of the PA government, a document summarizing a May 16, 2011, 3D Security Initiative briefing for a congressional staff audience stated that the PLC would not likely play an activist role—absent widespread consensus across factions—given the interim nature of a potential power-sharing agreement as a placeholder anticipating PA presidential and legislative elections.

[14] Consolidated Appropriations Act, 2008 (P.L. 110-161), "Economic Support Fund"; Omnibus Appropriations Act, 2009 (P.L. 111-8), §7040(f)(1).

[15] PLO Negotiations Affairs Department, "Q&A: Palestine's Accession to International Treaties," April 2, 2014, available at http://nad-plo.org/userfiles/file/fact%20sheets/Q&A%20Accession.pdf. The PLO claims that the status of the "State of Palestine" as a nonmember observer state of the United Nations—a status it received pursuant to U.N. General Assembly Resolution 67/19 in November 2012—entitles it to join a total of 63 treaties, conventions, and agencies, and that it "will do so in the best interests of its people, as and when it sees fit." For more information on this resolution and various Palestinian international initiatives, see CRS Report RL34074, *The Palestinians: Background and U.S. Relations*, by Jim Zanotti; CRS Report R43614, *Membership in the United Nations and Its Specialized Agencies*, by Luisa Blanchfield and Marjorie Ann Browne; and CRS Report R42999, *The United Nations Educational, Scientific, and Cultural Organization (UNESCO)*, by Luisa Blanchfield and Marjorie Ann Browne.

Another issue of congressional interest stems from allegations made by a number of observers that because money is fungible, U.S. aid to the PA indirectly supports PA payments supposedly going to some Palestinians (and/or their families) who are imprisoned for or accused of terrorism by Israel.[16] As a result, some Members of Congress are considering provisions that could reduce aid to the PA by an amount that the executive branch determines is used for the supposed PA payments in question (see "FY2015 Appropriations Process" below).

Moreover, because of congressional concerns that, among other things, U.S. funds might be diverted to Palestinian terrorist groups, aid to Palestinians is subject to a host of vetting and oversight requirements and legislative restrictions (see "Major Conditions, Limitations, and Restrictions on Aid" below). U.S. assistance to the Palestinians is given alongside assistance from other international donors, and U.S. policy makers routinely call for greater or more timely assistance from Arab governments in line with the pledges those governments make (see **Appendix B**). The figure below details recent direct budgetary assistance for the PA that the State Department has tracked from various sources of funding (i.e., states, international organizations, and other donors) from 2007 to 2014.

---

[16] See, e.g., Prepared testimony of Edwin Black, "Threats to Israel: Terrorist Funding and Trade Boycotts," House Committee on Foreign Affairs, Subcommittee on Terrorism, Nonproliferation, and Trade, March 5, 2014. As cited elsewhere in the report, Section 7039 of the Consolidated Appropriations Act, 2014 (P.L. 113-76) requires the Secretary of State to take all appropriate steps to ensure that ESF assistance for the West Bank and Gaza does not support terrorism, and to terminate assistance to "any individual, entity, or educational institution which the Secretary has determined to be involved in or advocating terrorist activity."

Figure 1. International Budget Support for the Palestinian Authority, 2007-2014

(by source of funding; current year $)

	2007	2008	2009	2010	2011	2012	2013	2014
Saudi Arabia	$127,704,197	$234,053,786	$241,056,731	$145,633,071	$179,693,900	$100,000,000	$260,265,649	$80,473,816
United Arab Emirates	$110,000,000	$134,221,750	$173,930,947	$42,906,703	$42,500,000	$85,486,120	$50,000,000	$0
Arab league	$0	$99,895	$0	$0	$0	$0	$0	$0
Oman	$0	$0	$2,909,431	$0	$10,000,000	$0	$5,000,000	$0
Algeria	$52,799,969	$62,943,959	$25,969,871	$29,574,309	$52,799,920	$26,400,000	$26,399,982	$26,399,960
Kuwait	$33,415,814	$80,000,000	$0	$50,000,000	$50,000,000	$50,000,000	$50,000,000	$0
Iraq	$10,000,000	$0	$0	$0	$0	$25,000,000	$28,749,980	$0
Egypt	$0	$14,628,676	$17,831,750	$7,895,200	$5,014,828	$3,175,861	$0	$0
Qatar	$110,076,873	$0	$0	$9,658,120	$0	$30,000,000	$8,999,982	$99,999,880
Arab League	**$443,996,853**	**$525,948,066**	**$461,698,730**	**$285,667,403**	**$340,008,648**	**$320,061,981**	**$429,415,593**	**$206,873,656**
EU PEGASE	$493,073,020	$651,272,444	$425,546,604	$382,233,417	$238,570,460	$267,418,287	$257,376,690	$75,733,016
France	$20,250,000	$37,162,854	$33,481,562	$30,374,246	$27,317,500	$24,130,000	$25,651,765	$0
Sweden	$2,933,280	$0	$0	$0	$0	$0	$0	$0
UK	$6,000,000	$57,200,000	$49,100,000	$76,900,000	$37,900,000	$35,580,000	$64,821,865	$19,000,000
Greece	$0	$0	$2,652,820	$2,800,000	$0	$0	$0	$0
Cyprus	$0	$0	$0	$100,000	$0	$0	$0	$0
Finland	$0	$3,600,000	$0	$0	$0	$0	$0	$0
Poland	$0	$500,000	$0	$0	$0	$0	$0	$0
EU and EU Members	**$522,256,300**	**$749,735,298**	**$510,780,986**	**$492,407,663**	**$303,787,960**	**$327,128,287**	**$347,850,320**	**$94,733,016**
United States	$4,705,897	$302,261,822	$275,000,000	$222,864,771	$50,000,000	$0	$348,000,000	$0
Other Donors	$41,069,651	$185,475,653	$100,709,599	$144,457,229	$67,898,799	$178,867,227	$125,699,960	$52,799,960
TOTAL	$1,012,028,701	$1,763,420,839	$1,348,189,315	$1,145,397,066	$761,695,407	$826,057,495	$1,250,965,873	$354,406,632

Source: U.S. State Department

Notes: All amounts are approximate. For information on the EU's PEGASE mechanism for channeling financial assistance to the PA from the EU budget and EU member states, see http://eeas.europa.eu/delegations/westbank/eu_westbank/tech_financial_cooperation/index_en.htm.

FY2015 Appropriations Process

Legislative Proposals

Conditions on Funding Hamas-Approved PA Government

The House version of the Department of State, Foreign Operations and Related Programs Appropriations Act, 2015 (H.R. 5013), as reported by the House Appropriations Committee in June 2014, features a provision (§7040(f)) that would differ from the P.L. 113-76 provision governing FY2014 aid to a power-sharing PA government. It would require any such government based on agreement with Hamas—possibly including the current PA government—to meet the Section 620K principles (cited above) without reference to the question of "undue influence." In explaining this provision, H.Rept. 113-499 stated that funds will be prohibited "to any power-sharing government that is based on agreement with Hamas, unless conditions required in the Palestinian Anti-terrorism Act of 2006 (PATA) are met." The report further stated that:

> The Committee has not allocated funds for the Palestinian Authority [for FY2015] because the current government was put in place based on an agreement with Hamas. The Committee

has, therefore, deferred the decision to provide funds until it can be determined that such government is actually adhering to the requirements included in the PATA.

The Senate version (S. 2499), as reported by the Senate Appropriations Committee in June 2014, would maintain the provision for FY2015 in the same form as it exists for FY2014. However, S.Rept. 113-195 would direct the Secretary of State to submit a report to the committee prior to obligating FY2015 ESF assistance for the West Bank and Gaza "detailing and assessing the capabilities of the Palestinian Authority to manage and conduct effective oversight of U.S. assistance in accordance with section 7040(f)."

On April 29, 2014, Senator Rand Paul introduced the Stand with Israel Act of 2014 (S. 2265),[17] which would prohibit U.S. assistance to the PA,[18] subject to an exception for any particular fiscal year if the President certifies during that fiscal year that the PA has satisfied a number of conditions.[19]

Funding Reduction for PA Payments to Alleged Terrorists

Both H.R. 5013 (§7041(j)(3)) and S. 2499 (§7041(i)(3)) include a provision that would require the Secretary of State to reduce ESF made available for the PA by an amount the Secretary determines "is equivalent to that expended by the Palestinian Authority in payments to individuals and the families of such individuals that are imprisoned for acts of terrorism or who died committing such acts during the previous calendar year."[20] H.R. 5013 would also require a report to the Committees on Appropriations on the amount reduced for FY2015 prior to the obligation of funds for the PA, and on the steps taken to prevent any such payments by the PA.

A July 1, 2014, *Washington Times* column asserted that the PA has announced that prisoner payments might be shifted from the PA to the PLO. The column quoted a PA spokesman as saying on television in June 2014 that the shift would "provide political and legal cover" and "eliminate arguments ... that [foreign] aid money [to the PA] is going to the prisoners."[21] It is unclear whether or how such a shift might affect the proposed legislation discussed above.

---

[17] The act has garnered at least 17 co-sponsors and has been referred to the Senate Foreign Relations Committee.

[18] In appraising S. 2265, one journalist stated that "a former U.S. official critical of the administration explained that the bill is dangerous insofar as 'it denies any flexibility in areas where flexibility is of great importance for Israeli security. It would mean zero funding of any Palestinian security service, even if that service is doing yeoman work against Hamas and works secretly hand in glove with Israel to stop terror against Israelis. Why is that smart?'" Jennifer Rubin, "Rand Paul gets it partially right on aid to the PA," *Washington Post*, April 30, 2014.

[19] The conditions are (1) formally recognizing the right of Israel to exist as a Jewish state, (2) publicly recognizing the state of Israel, (3) renouncing terrorism, (4) purging all individuals with terrorist ties from security services, (5) terminating funding of anti-American and anti-Israel incitement, (6) publicly pledging to not engage in war with Israel, and (7) honoring previous diplomatic agreements. H.Res. 622, which was introduced by Representative Trent Franks and has garnered at least 23 co-sponsors, would call for the PA to dissolve the "unity government with Hamas" and take a number of conciliatory measures vis-à-vis Israel, while, if no dissolution occurs, calling for the Secretary of State to designate both the PA and the PLO as Foreign Terrorist Organizations.

[20] H.Res. 542, which was introduced by Representative Ted Yoho and has garnered at least 10 co-sponsors, would express the sense of the House that U.S. aid to the PA should be suspended until the PA stops making such payments.

[21] Clifford D. May, quoting PA spokesperson Ehab Bessaiso, "MAY: Salaries for terrorists," *Washington Times*, July 1, 2014.

Exclusion of PA from Defense Appropriations

The Department of Defense Appropriations Act, 2015 (H.R. 4870), which passed the House in June 2014, contained provisions that would prohibit funds made available by the act from being obligated to the PA (§10033) or from being used to transfer weapons to the PA (§10024).

Possible Questions for Congress

- Is aid to the Palestinians in the U.S. national interest? If so, what specific policy outcomes should Congress seek to achieve or avoid by providing or not providing various types and levels of aid? How important for the United States is aid to the Palestinians among other budget priorities, both foreign and domestic?

- The basic outlines of U.S. aid to the Palestinians have remained relatively constant from FY2008 to the present. How effective has aid been during this time in achieving desired U.S. policy outcomes or avoiding undesirable outcomes? What utility will various types and levels of aid likely provide in light of Israeli-Palestinian and broader regional developments that have taken place since FY2008, including in recent months and years?

- Should a "power of approval" by Hamas over a PA government, absent any further level of participation, trigger a requirement for that government's acceptance and compliance with the Section 620K principles discussed above?

- Should U.S. restrictions be relaxed, tightened, or kept as is regarding which Palestinian party/ies is/are answerable for accepting and complying with the Section 620K principles?

- Should Congress grant the President discretion—under certain conditions and/or for specific purposes—to waive aid restrictions relating to a PA government that includes or involves Hamas but does not meet the Section 620K principles?

- What are the potential costs and benefits of reducing, delaying, suspending, or ending aid in reprisal for Palestinian actions taken in direct opposition to stated U.S. policies? Would the assumption of greater responsibility for Palestinian assistance by other international and regional actors serve or run counter to U.S. interests?[22]

- How effective has U.S. security assistance to the PA been? Under what circumstances can the United States, Israel, and the Palestinian people rely on the

---

[22] One possible reason that some Members of Congress have shown reluctance to continue funding the PA in light of Palestinian initiatives within the U.N. system is a possible perception of these Palestinian initiatives as an attempt to undermine the U.S. role as "honest broker" and guarantor of the peace process. U.S. lawmakers and officials also may view Palestinian action in international fora as a sign that U.S. attempts to use aid for political leverage with the Palestinians are unproductive. However, in testimony offered to the House Committee on Foreign Affairs, Subcommittee on the Middle East and North Africa, on May 8, 2014, Jonathan Schanzer of the Foundation for Defense of Democracies said, in addressing the possible consequences of a U.S. aid cutoff to the Palestinians, "You know, if we zero out Palestinian funding, then here is the big problem. You are going to have someone else come in and they are going to be worse. More than likely, you are going to see the Saudis, the Iranians, the Qataris, the Turks. They are all going to come in and they are not even going to hold the Palestinians to account at all. The important thing from my perspective, if we are going to keep the funding going, we need to make sure that we have tighter controls. We need to demand performance. And, in my opinion, we have just simply failed to do so."

PA security forces to counter terrorism and maintain law and order? Do questions regarding the professionalism and staying power of other Western-trained forces in the region (such as in Iraq) also apply to PA forces?

- What additional legislative and oversight measures, if any, should Congress take to prevent aid from being used—or allegations that it is being used—to support Palestinian terrorism? Should such measures address payments made by the PA and/or other Palestinian organizations to Palestinians (and/or their families) who are imprisoned for or accused of terrorism by Israel?

- There are a number of factors—economic, political, educational, security—that Congress might consider when determining if and how to provide aid to Palestinians in Gaza. Which of these are most significant? Do recent changes in Gaza create a more or less advantageous situation for U.S. aid initiatives, given Hamas's relinquishment of day-to-day control but maintenance of its militia and rocket arsenal, as well as changes and continued uncertainty in Egypt and its Sinai Peninsula (which adjoins Gaza)?

- Does U.S. aid to the Palestinians strengthen leaders who support peaceful coexistence with Israel, and if so, how? Does it undermine them, and if so, how? Should Congress and the Obama Administration seek to strengthen or stabilize the rule of Mahmoud Abbas and his colleagues despite charges of corruption and growing authoritarianism in their circles?[23]

- How much of a role should the United States play in supporting Palestinian democracy, institutional reform, rule of law, and economic development? What are prospects for these efforts following the June 2013 replacement of former PA prime minister Salam Fayyad?

- How should Congress evaluate the costs and benefits of UNRWA's activities, and how, if at all, should this affect U.S. contributions to UNRWA?

- In crafting legislation and providing oversight of executive branch action, should Congress consider the possible occurrence of high-impact events—such as a major terrorist attack or uprising, a surprise election outcome, an outbreak of war, or pursuit by Palestinians of political strategies outside of negotiations with Israel? If so, how should this consideration shape congressional initiatives?

---

[23] Some allegations of PA corruption focus on the Palestine Investment Fund (PIF). The Government Accountability Office (GAO) published a July 2013 report on U.S. involvement with the PIF in response to a request from Representatives Nita Lowey, Steve Israel, and Ted Deutch. The report stated that USAID has provided $1.3 million in project assistance to an international school in Gaza that is owned by a PIF subsidiary, and that USAID and the U.S. Overseas Private Investment Corporation (OPIC) have provided assistance and/or loan guarantees to a West Bank mortgage lending corporation and a West Bank loan guarantee facility that PIF also supports. GAO, *U.S. Programs Involving the Palestine Investment Fund*, GAO Foreign Assistance Report 13-457, July 2013.

Major Conditions, Limitations, and Restrictions on Aid

Annual appropriations legislation routinely contains the following conditions, limitations, and restrictions on U.S. aid to Palestinians (for conditions regarding a "power-sharing government" involving Hamas, see "Current and Past Legislative Conditions" above):[24]

- *Hamas and Terrorism*: Aid is specifically prohibited from going to Hamas or Hamas-controlled entities, and no aid may be made available for the purpose of recognizing or otherwise honoring individuals who commit or have committed acts of terrorism. Additionally, the Secretary of State is required to take all appropriate steps to ensure that ESF assistance for the West Bank and Gaza does not support terrorism, and to terminate assistance to "any individual, entity, or educational institution which the Secretary has determined to be involved in or advocating terrorist activity."[25]

- *Palestinian Membership in the United Nations or U.N. Specialized Agencies, and Action at the International Criminal Court (ICC)*: No Economic Support Fund aid is permitted to the PA if the Palestinians:

  1. obtain from this point forward (the restriction does not apply to Palestinian membership in UNESCO) "the same standing as member states or full membership as a state in the United Nations or any specialized agency thereof outside an agreement negotiated between Israel and the Palestinians";[26] or

  2. initiate "an International Criminal Court judicially authorized investigation, or actively support such an investigation, that subjects Israeli nationals to an investigation for alleged crimes against Palestinians."[27]

  The Secretary of State may waive both restrictions for national security reasons by filing a waiver detailing how "the continuation of assistance would assist in furthering Middle East peace."[28]

- *PA Personnel in Gaza*: No aid is permitted for PA personnel located in Gaza. Although the PA does pay salaries to individuals located in Gaza, USAID insists that U.S. direct budgetary assistance to the PA goes toward paying the PA's suppliers and commercial creditors (see "Direct Assistance to the Palestinian Authority" below).

- *PLO and Palestinian Broadcasting Corporation (PBC)*: No aid is permitted for the PLO or for the PBC.

---

[24] Current conditions and restrictions for FY2014 are contained in P.L. 113-76, §§7036-7040 and 7041(j).

[25] P.L. 113-76, §7039.

[26] P.L. 113-76, §7041(j)(2). Because U.N. General Assembly Resolution 67/19, which was adopted in November 2012, did not provide member state status to "Palestine" at the United Nations (it only conferred nonmember state observer status), it did not trigger the aid restriction.

[27] P.L. 113-76, §7041(j)(2).

[28] Ibid.

- *Palestinian State*: No funds may be provided to support a future Palestinian state unless the Secretary of State certifies that the governing entity of the state:

  1. has demonstrated a firm commitment to peaceful coexistence with the State of Israel;

  2. is taking appropriate measures to counter terrorism and terrorist financing in the West Bank and Gaza in cooperation with Israel and others; and

  3. is working with other countries in the region to "vigorously pursue efforts to establish a just, lasting, and comprehensive peace in the Middle East that will enable Israel and an independent Palestinian state to exist within the context of full and normal relationships."[29]

  This restriction does not apply to aid meant to reform the Palestinian governing entity so that it might meet the three conditions outlined above. Additionally, the President is permitted to waive this restriction for national security purposes.

- *Vetting, Monitoring, and Evaluation*: As discussed throughout this report, for U.S. aid programs for the Palestinians, annual appropriations legislation routinely requires executive branch reports and certifications, as well as internal and Government Accountability Office (GAO) audits. These requirements appear to be aimed at, among other things, preventing U.S. aid from benefitting terrorists or abetting corruption, and assessing aid programs' effectiveness.[30]

Types of U.S. Bilateral Aid to the Palestinians

Project Assistance (Economic Support Fund)

Types of Funding Programs

Most economic aid to the Palestinians is appropriated through the ESF account and provided by USAID and, to a far lesser degree, the State Department[31] to implementing partners (both for-profit and nonprofit contractors) operating in the West Bank and the Gaza Strip. Funds are allocated in this program for projects in sectors such as humanitarian assistance, economic development, democratic reform, improving water access and other infrastructure, health care, education, and vocational training. Currently most, if not all, funds for the Gaza Strip are dedicated to humanitarian assistance and economic recovery needs.[32] In addition to bilateral U.S.

---

[29] P.L. 113-76, §7036(a).

[30] See, e.g., P.L. 113-76, §§7039-7040. GAO audits are available on the following U.S. aid programs to the Palestinians: (1) Economic Support Fund, including direct assistance to the PA and project assistance (audit for FY2010-FY2011 accessible at http://www.gao.gov/assets/600/592431.pdf), (2) security assistance to the PA through the International Narcotics Control and Law Enforcement account (http://www.gao.gov/new.items/d10505.pdf), and (3) contributions to UNRWA through the Migration and Refugee Assistance and Emergency Refugee and Migration Assistance accounts (http://www.gao.gov/new.items/d09622.pdf).

[31] For example, see the State Department's Middle East Partnership Initiative (MEPI) West Bank/Gaza website at http://mepi.state.gov/where-we-work2/west-bank--gaza html. As stated on USAID's U.S. Overseas Loans and Grants website (http://gbk.eads.usaidallnet.gov), additional amounts have been provided to Palestinians in the West Bank and Gaza via the Department of Agriculture and miscellaneous grant programs.

[32] For further detail on the types of projects funded, see GAO, *U.S. Assistance to the West Bank and Gaza for Fiscal* (continued...)

---

assistance to the Palestinians, some amounts generally are allocated from various foreign assistance accounts for Israeli-Palestinian reconciliation or Arab-Israeli cooperation.[33]

Vetting Requirements and Procedures

USAID's West Bank and Gaza program is subject to a specialized vetting process (for non-U.S. organizations and individuals) and to yearly audits intended to ensure that funds are not diverted to Hamas or other organizations classified as terrorist groups by the U.S. government.[34] This vetting process has become more rigorous since around 2008-2009, presumably in response to allegations that U.S. economic assistance was indirectly supporting Palestinian terrorist groups, and following an internal audit in which USAID reportedly concluded it could not "reasonably ensure" that its money would not wind up in terrorist hands.[35]

A February 2009 statement from USAID described its revamped vetting procedures as follows:

> All NGOs applying for grants from USAID are required to certify, before award of the grant will be made, that they do not provide material support to terrorists.... Before making an award of either a contract or a grant to a local NGO, the USAID West Bank/Gaza Mission checks the organization and its principal officers, directors and other key personnel against lists maintained by the Office of Foreign Assets Control (OFAC) within the U.S. Department of Treasury. The Mission also checks these organizations and individuals through law enforcement and intelligence community systems accessed by USAID's Office of Security. At present, the Mission collects additional information up front in addition to the individual's full [four-part] name, such as a government issued photo-ID number and the individual's date and place of birth.... [USAID's] West Bank/Gaza program possess[es] the most comprehensive partner vetting system for foreign assistance throughout the U.S. Government.[36]

(...continued)

Years 2010 and 2011, GAO Foreign Assistance Report 12-81, July 13, 2012.

[33] In past years Congress has generally recommended that an annual amount from the ESF and Development Assistance accounts ($10 million in FY2012) be put toward a "New Generation in the Middle East" initiative to "build understanding, tolerance, and mutual respect among the next generation of Israeli and Palestinian leaders." P.L. 112-74, §7062(f)(2). P.L. 113-76 did not contain a similarly explicit recommendation for FY2014, though §7060(f) did earmark $26 million for reconciliation programs generally. Moreover, appropriations of a few million dollars annually generally go toward (1) USAID's Conflict Management and Mitigation Israeli-Palestinian people to people programs, out of the Bureau of Democracy, Conflict, and Humanitarian Assistance budget; and (2) the Middle East Multilaterals and Middle East Regional Cooperation programs, which support Arab-Israeli cooperation in various research and technical fields.

[34] P.L. 113-76, §7039(b) sets forth the legal requirements for vetting: "Prior to the obligation of funds appropriated by this Act under the heading `Economic Support Fund' for assistance for the West Bank and Gaza, the Secretary of State shall take all appropriate steps to ensure that such assistance is not provided to or through any individual, private or government entity, or educational institution that the Secretary knows or has reason to believe advocates, plans, sponsors, engages in, or has engaged in, terrorist activity nor, with respect to private entities or educational institutions, those that have as a principal officer of the entity's governing board or governing board of trustees any individual that has been determined to be involved in, or advocating terrorist activity or determined to be a member of a designated foreign terrorist organization: *Provided*, That the Secretary of State shall, as appropriate, establish procedures specifying the steps to be taken in carrying out this subsection and shall terminate assistance to any individual, entity, or educational institution which the Secretary has determined to be involved in or advocating terrorist activity."

[35] Jim Tankersley, "Audit: Terrorists Got U.S. Aid; Agency's Screening Called Inadequate," *Chicago Tribune*, November 16, 2007; See also Testimony of Henrietta Fore, then USAID Administrator and Director of U.S. Foreign Assistance, House Appropriations Subcommittee on State, Foreign Operations, and Related Programs Hearing on the Fiscal 2009 Budget for the U.S. Agency for International Development, February 27, 2008.

[36] Statement issued by USAID to CRS on February 5, 2009. USAID does not subject U.S. organizations to vetting due (continued...)

A May 2009 GAO report found that USAID had strengthened its antiterrorism policies and procedures in response to recommendations GAO had made in a 2006 report.[37]

Direct Assistance to the Palestinian Authority (Economic Support Fund)

Budgetary assistance is a major part of the U.S. strategy to support the PA in the West Bank, although some Members of Congress have voiced expectations of better governance and a more proactive approach by the PA toward peace with Israel in return.[38] According to annual foreign operations appropriations laws, congressionally approved funds for the West Bank and Gaza Strip cannot be given directly to the PA unless the President submits a waiver to Congress stating that doing so is in the interest of national security, and the Secretary of State certifies that (1) there is a single PA treasury account, civil service roster, and payroll; and (2) "the Palestinian Authority is acting to counter incitement of violence against Israelis and is supporting activities aimed at promoting peace, coexistence, and security cooperation with Israel."[39]

As mentioned above, annual appropriations legislation also routinely places conditions on aid to any power-sharing PA government "of which Hamas is a member," and, since FY2012, appropriations legislation has extended these conditions to any PA government that results from an agreement with Hamas over which Hamas has "undue influence." Even after money is transferred to the PA's treasury account, the United States retains prior approval of any transactions from that account, along with a power of audit over those funds and a three-year right of refund.[40]

During the final year of President George W. Bush's Administration, President Bush issued waivers providing $300 million in direct budgetary assistance to the PA. President Barack Obama

---

(...continued)

to U.S. privacy law concerns. See GAO, *Measures to Prevent Inadvertent Payments to Terrorists Under Palestinian Aid Programs Have Been Strengthened, but Some Weaknesses Remain*, GAO Foreign Assistance Report 09-622, May 2009.

[37] See GAO, *Measures to Prevent Inadvertent Payments to Terrorists...*, op. cit. A schematic detailing USAID's vetting process is found on page 42 of the report. GAO did recommend in the report that USAID take steps to ensure that it and its primary contractors use the same rigor at the subcontractor level that they employed in requiring antiterrorism clauses and certifications during their contracting process.

[38] Representative Ileana Ros-Lehtinen, Chairman of the House Foreign Affairs Committee's Subcommittee on the Middle East and North Africa, voiced significant concern over the Administration's provision of direct budgetary assistance to the PA when serving as ranking Member of the full committee in November 2010: "It is deeply disturbing that the Administration is continuing to bail out the Palestinian leadership when they continue to fail to meet their commitments, under international agreements and requirements outlined in U.S. law, including dismantling the Palestinian terrorist infrastructure, combating corruption, stopping anti-Israel and anti-Semitic incitement, and recognizing Israel's right to exist as a Jewish state." House Foreign Affairs Committee website: "Ros-Lehtinen Opposes Latest U.S. 'Bailout' Installment for Palestinian Authority," November 11, 2010.

[39] See P.L. 113-76, §7040 ("Limitation on Assistance for the Palestinian Authority"). In the event of a presidential waiver, §7040(d) requires the President to submit a report to the Committees on Appropriations "detailing the justification for the waiver, the purposes for which the funds will be spent, and the accounting procedures in place to ensure that the funds are properly disbursed: *Provided*, That the report shall also detail the steps the Palestinian Authority has taken to arrest terrorists, confiscate weapons and dismantle the terrorist infrastructure."

[40] USAID FY2013 Congressional Notification #93, July 29, 2013.

has followed the precedent Bush established by authorizing a total of $898 million in direct budgetary assistance, as follows:

- In July 2009, $200 million in ESF money were transferred to the PA in the wake of a presidential waiver issued by President Obama.[41]

- In December 2009, $75 million in budgetary assistance were provided to the PA under the July presidential waiver as an advance on FY2010 ESF funds, pursuant to a continuing resolution (later appropriated pursuant to P.L. 111-117).

- In April 2010, another $75 million in budgetary assistance from the ESF account were provided to the PA following a presidential waiver.[42]

- In October 2010, $150 million in budgetary assistance were provided to the PA following a presidential waiver as an advance on FY2011 ESF funds, pursuant to the Continuing Appropriations Act, 2011 (P.L. 111-242).[43]

- In September 2011, $50 million in budgetary assistance from the ESF account were provided following a presidential waiver.[44]

- In April 2012, the Administration notified Congress of its intention to obligate an additional $200 million in budgetary assistance from the ESF account, accompanied by a presidential waiver.[45] However, due to delays from informal congressional holds, this amount was ultimately reprogrammed for project assistance. In February 2013, $200 million in FY2013 ESF funding were provided following a presidential waiver[46] to replace the reprogrammed amount.

- Another $148 million in budgetary assistance from the ESF account were provided following a July 2013 presidential waiver.[47]

Direct U.S. budgetary assistance to the PA goes toward paying off its commercial debt, as the following FY2013 USAID congressional notification language says:

> Direct budget support will be used in the same manner as previous transfers—to service debt to commercial suppliers and commercial banks. Debt to commercial banks will be debt originally incurred for purchases from commercial suppliers. Each of the payees will have been vetted in accordance with USAID West Bank and Gaza existing procedures, as applicable, as a precondition to the transfer of funds by the PA for such payments. Funds may also be used to pay for upcoming purchases from commercial suppliers or reimbursements of recent purchases from suppliers.[48]

---

[41] Presidential Determination 2009-23.

[42] Presidential Memorandum 2010-06.

[43] Presidential Determination 2011-1.

[44] USAID FY2011 Congressional Notification #133, August 18, 2011; Presidential Determination 2011-14, August 30, 2011.

[45] USAID FY2012 Congressional Notification #47, April 27, 2012; Presidential Memorandum, April 25, 2012.

[46] USAID FY2013 Congressional Notification #25, February 1, 2013; Presidential Memorandum—Presidential Determination Regarding Waiver of Restriction on Providing Funds to the Palestinian Authority, February 8, 2013.

[47] USAID FY2013 Congressional Notification #93, July 29, 2013; Presidential Memorandum—Waiver of Restriction on Providing Funds to the Palestinian Authority, July 26, 2013.

[48] USAID FY2013 Congressional Notification #93, July 29, 2013.

As mentioned above, despite this explanation of U.S. budgetary assistance to the PA, allegations routinely surface that the fungible nature of funding means that U.S. aid indirectly supports PA payments, including those supposedly going to some Palestinians (and/or their families) who are imprisoned for or accused of terrorism by Israel.[49]

U.S. Security Assistance to the Palestinian Authority

Aid from the INCLE account has been given to train, reform, advise, house, and provide nonlethal equipment for PA civil security forces in the West Bank loyal to President Abbas. This aid is aimed at countering militants from organizations such as Hamas and Palestine Islamic Jihad – Shaqaqi Faction, and establishing the rule of law for an expected Palestinian state. In recent years, some of this training and infrastructure assistance has been provided to strengthen and reform the PA criminal justice sector. Regarding FY2014 assistance, according to July 3, 2014, email correspondence from a State Department official to CRS:

> We plan to notify and obligate [FY2014 INCLE] funds later this year; but the timing will depend on our assessment of the actions, policies, and composition of the interim PA government and its continued adherence to Quartet principles. The planned breakdown for FY 2014 funds includes roughly $45 million to train and equip the PA Security Forces; $13.9 million for justice, corrections, and law enforcement programs; and $4.5 million for strategic development and capacity building in the Ministry of Interior.

After Hamas forcibly took control of the Gaza Strip in June 2007, the office of the U.S. Security Coordinator (USSC) for Israel and the Palestinian Authority (a three-star U.S. general/flag officer, supported by U.S. and allied staff and military officers from the United Kingdom, Canada, and around six other countries) has worked in coordination with the State Department's Bureau of International Narcotics and Law Enforcement Affairs (INL) to sponsor and oversee training for West Bank-based PA security forces personnel, many of whom have been newly recruited. From 2007 to 2012, nine full PA National Security Forces (NSF)[50] special battalions and two Presidential Guard (PG)[51] battalions—constituting more than 6,000 total personnel—received initial training at the Jordan International Police Training Center (JIPTC).[52] Additionally, hundreds of members of the PA Civil Defense (firefighters and other emergency responders) have been trained in Amman at the Jordanian Academy of Civil Protection.[53]

Following the completion of initial training for newly formed PA security force battalions, the USSC/INL program reportedly shifted to a less resource intensive "advise and assist" role

---

[49] See, e.g., Prepared testimony of Edwin Black, op. cit.

[50] The NSF (with approximately 8,000 active personnel), the organization that receives the greatest amount of training and other resources as a result of U.S. INCLE assistance, is considered by many Palestinians to be analogous to a national army—housed in barracks, classified by military rank, and subject to a military-style command structure.

[51] The PG's main purposes are to protect the PA President and other VIPs, to respond to crises, and to protect official PA facilities.

[52] Neither NSF nor PG personnel possess the legal authority to make arrests when tasked with law and order missions. Therefore, they generally operate as strategic reinforcements and force protection for the organizations empowered to make arrests—the Palestinian Civil Police (PCP, with approximately 7,200 active personnel) and two intelligence organizations (the Preventive Security Organization and the General Intelligence Service) that are less visible than the PCP and NSF in day-to-day law and order tasks.

[53] The information in this paragraph on PA security forces training in Jordan was provided to CRS on January 14, 2013, by a senior Western official based in the region.

alongside its efforts to assist the PA in improving the functioning of its criminal justice system. The self-described USSC/INL role is to help PA security forces "develop indigenous readiness, training, and logistics programs and the capability to maintain/sustain their force structure readiness and infrastructure."[54]

The USSC/INL security assistance program exists alongside other assistance and training programs provided to Palestinian security forces and intelligence organizations by various other countries and the European Union (EU).[55] Some reports cite the probable existence of covert U.S. assistance programs as well.[56] By most accounts, the PA forces receiving training have shown increased professionalism and have helped substantially improve law and order and lower the profile of terrorist organizations in West Bank cities.[57] Israeli officials generally support the USSC/INL program, routinely citing both the PA forces' greater effectiveness as well as increased and sustained levels of Israel-PA security cooperation in the West Bank since the program began. This cooperation, however, is vulnerable to criticism from Hamas and others seeking to undermine Mahmoud Abbas's popular credibility as a champion of Palestinian national aspirations.[58]

Additionally, the aspiration to coordinate international security assistance efforts and to consolidate the various PA security forces under unified civilian control that is accountable to rule of law and to human rights norms remains largely unfulfilled. PA forces have come under criticism for the political targeting of Hamas—in collaboration with Israel and the United States—through massive shutdowns and forced leadership changes to West Bank charities with alleged ties to Hamas members and through reportedly arbitrary detentions of Hamas members and supporters.[59] Also, since 2012, some PA security personnel have reportedly been involved in criminal activity in a way that has raised questions about the sustainability of law and order in parts of the northern West Bank that have been held out as models of progress. This reportedly mainly involved personnel who had been granted amnesty from previous involvement with terrorist groups. At least one report cited unnamed Palestinian officials asserting that those arrested by the PA for criminal activity included a few personnel who belonged to battalions that had received U.S.-backed training.[60] Some of those arrested reportedly "claimed to have been

---

[54] Testimony of Lieutenant General Michael Moeller, then U.S. Security Coordinator for Israel and the PA, Hearing of the House Committee on Foreign Affairs, Subcommittee on the Middle East and South Asia, July 12, 2011.

[55] In January 2006, the EU Coordinating Office for Palestinian Police Support (EUPOL COPPS) was launched to help train and equip the Palestinian Civil Police. EUPOL COPPS also advises the PA on criminal justice and rule of law issues. EUPOL COPPS has 71 international staff and 41 local hires in the West Bank, and an annual operating budget of approximately €9.57 million. See http://eupolcopps.eu.

[56] See, e.g., Yezid Sayigh, *Policing the People, Building the State: Authoritarian Transformation in the West Bank and Gaza*, Carnegie Endowment for International Peace, February 2011; Ian Cobain, "CIA working with Palestinian security agents," *guardian.co.uk*, December 17, 2009.

[57] Improvements in the PA security forces' leadership and capacity may factor into Israeli data that—according to information a senior Western official based in the region provided to CRS on June 12, 2012—cited a 96% decrease in West Bank terrorist attacks since 2007. Other factors contributing to the decline in terrorism may include enhanced Israeli security measures, Palestinian fatigue with or decreasing appetite for politically motivated violence or popular resistance, and various political and economic incentives and other developments.

[58] For example, Abbas's public statements in June 2014 at an Organization of Islamic Cooperation meeting in Saudi Arabia in support of security coordination with Israel to find three missing Israeli youth in the West Bank (who were later found dead) have attracted widespread popular criticism and protest, and even isolated instances of violence, including against PA security forces.

[59] See, e.g., Nathan Thrall, "Our Man in Palestine," *New York Review of Books*, October 14, 2010.

[60] See, e.g., Karin Brulliard, "Drama in West Bank city of Jenin shows cracks in Palestinian nation-building project," (continued...)

humiliated and tortured by their colleagues in the security forces and placed in cells with Hamas members against whom they had fought years earlier."[61]

Some Palestinians and outside observers assert that the effectiveness and credibility of PA operations are undermined by Israeli restrictions—including curfews, checkpoints, no-go zones, and limitations on international arms and equipment transfers—as well as by Israel's own security operations in the West Bank[62] and at crossings into Gaza. Israel claims that its continuing operations in the West Bank are necessary in order to reduce the threat of terrorism. It is unclear how concerns about the effectiveness of the PA security forces might evolve if protests and occasional instances of Israeli-Palestinian confrontation in the West Bank increase in frequency and intensity amid heightened tension.

Moreover, in a June 2014 speech, Israeli Prime Minister Binyamin Netanyahu expressed skepticism regarding the ability of local Western-trained forces to keep Islamist militants at bay:

> [A challenge] we face is to stabilize the area west of the Jordan River security line. In this area of the West Bank no force can guarantee Israel's security other than the [Israel Defense Forces] and our security services. Time after time we have seen how the local forces trained by the West to stop the Islamists cannot be relied upon following the departure of those Western forces. This is what happened with the Lebanese army vis-à-vis Hezbollah following Israel's departure from Lebanon; this is what happened in Gaza when the Palestinian Authority forces were defeated by Hamas after Israel's withdrawal; and this is what is happening now in Iraq following the departure of American forces.[63]

How the newly formed government via Fatah-Hamas agreement may affect the activities of PA security forces in the West Bank is unclear, though it is possible that these activities will remain largely unchanged until either PA presidential and legislative elections can be held or Fatah and Hamas can agree on security coordination for both the West Bank and Gaza. The likelihood of either contingency occurring is seriously questioned by many observers.

U.S. Contributions to UNRWA

Overview

The United States is the largest single-state donor to UNRWA. According to UNRWA's website, its mandate from the U.N. General Assembly is to "provide relief, human development and protection services to Palestine refugees and persons displaced by the 1967 hostilities in its fields

---

(...continued)

Washington Post, May 25, 2012.

[61] International Crisis Group, *Buying Time? Money, Guns and Politics in the West Bank*, Middle East Report No. 142, May 29, 2013.

[62] These operations underscore the fact that the Israeli-Palestinian agreements that authorized the creation of Palestinian security forces in the 1990s in areas of limited Palestinian self-rule contained clauses that preserved Israel's prerogative to conduct operations in those areas for purposes of its own security.

[63] Translated transcript of remarks by Prime Minister Netanyahu at the Institute for National Security Studies, Tel Aviv, Israel, June 29, 2014.

of operation: Jordan, Lebanon, the Syrian Arab Republic, West Bank and the Gaza Strip."[64] "Palestine refugees" include original refugees from the 1948 Arab-Israeli War and their descendants—now comprising approximately 5 million Palestinians in the places listed above. U.S. contributions to UNRWA—separate from U.S. bilateral aid to the West Bank and Gaza— come from the Migration and Refugee Assistance (MRA) account and, in exceptional situations, the Emergency Refugee and Migration Assistance (ERMA) account, which are managed by the State Department's Bureau of Population, Refugees, and Migration (PRM). Since UNRWA's inception in 1950, the United States has provided the agency with more than $4.9 billion in contributions (see **Table 2** below). Other refugees worldwide fall under the mandate of the U.N. High Commissioner for Refugees (UNHCR).

The budget for UNRWA's core activities (general fund) for 2014 is approximately $732 million, funded mainly by Western governments, international organizations, and private donors.[65] Core activities include providing food, shelter, education, medical care, and other humanitarian services to designated beneficiaries. In December 2013, the organization, which is primarily funded by voluntary donor contributions, projected a revenue shortfall for 2014 of $65 million.[66] Financial difficulties and resulting employee layoffs and service reductions have at least partly contributed to protests and strikes in the West Bank and Gaza.[67] UNRWA also creates special emergency funds for pressing humanitarian needs. U.S. contributions totaled $294.0 million for FY2013 ($135.1 million for the general fund, $158.9 million for emergency funds and additional activities).[68] According to CRS email correspondence with PRM, $250.9 million in FY2014 contributions have been disbursed as of July 1, 2014 ($135.4 million for the general fund, $115.5 million for emergency funds and additional activities).

---

[64] According to a 2010 article by the chief of UNRWA's international law division, "UNRWA does not have a constituent instrument (unlike the World Health Organization [WHO]) or a statute (unlike the Office of the United Nations High Commissioner for Refugees [UNHCR]); its mandate is not conveniently stated in one place and must be derived from all relevant resolutions and requests." Lance Bartholomeusz, "The Mandate of UNRWA at Sixty," *Refugee Survey Quarterly*, vol. 28, nos. 2 and 3, 2010.

[65] According to statistics culled from UNRWA's website, U.S. contributions in 2012 constituted approximately 20% of the UNRWA General Fund budget and 26% of the total budget. Aggregate contributions from the European Commission and European states (including both EU members and nonmembers) and regions constituted approximately 56% of the total budget. Aggregate contributions from Muslim-majority countries and Muslim organizations constituted approximately 9% of the total budget.

[66] U.N. General Assembly press release, "As Budget Shortfall, Insecurity Threaten Efforts of UN Agency For Palestine Refugees, 17 Member States Promise Funds at Pledging Conference," December 3, 2013.

[67] See, e.g., "UNRWA: More talks after union ends strike," *Ma'an,* January 27, 2014.

[68] CRS email correspondence with State Department official, September 30, 2013. According to this correspondence, "$75,000,000 [of the FY2013 contributions were allocated] for Emergency Appeal for the West Bank and Gaza, $3,000,000 for "Restoring Dignity" appeal for Lebanon, which assists Nahr al Bared residents who remain displaced, $10,000,000 for Gaza reconstruction, and $70,900,000 for emergency needs in Syria, Lebanon, and Jordan resulting from the conflict in Syria."

Table 2. Historical U.S. Government Contributions to UNRWA

(in $ millions)

Fiscal Year(s)	Amount	Fiscal Year(s)	Amount
1950-1989	1,473.3	2002	119.3
1990	57.0	2003	134.0
1991	75.6	2004	127.4
1992	69.0	2005	108.0
1993	73.8	2006	137.0
1994	78.2	2007	154.2
1995	74.8	2008	184.7
1996	77.0	2009	268.0
1997	79.2	2010	237.8
1998	78.3	2011	249.4
1999	80.5	2012	233.3
2000	89.0	2013	294.0
2001	123.0	2014	250.9
		TOTAL	**4,926.7**

Source: U.S. State Department.

Notes: All amounts are approximate.

Until the 1990s, Arab governments refrained from contributing to UNRWA's budget in an effort to keep the Palestinian refugee issue on the international agenda and to press Israel to accept responsibility for their plight. Since then, several Arab states have made relatively modest annual contributions toward UNRWA's core activities. According to one UNRWA official, some Arab states, notably Saudi Arabia and Kuwait, have given "very generously to emergencies—like Syria today and Gaza and Lebanon in the past—and to special construction (housing) projects."[69]

In Gaza, most observers acknowledge that the role of UNRWA in providing basic services (i.e., food, health care, education) takes much of the burden off the PA and Hamas personnel who officially or unofficially hold sway in the territory in either a governing or a security capacity. As a result, some complain that this amounts to UNRWA's enabling of the Palestinians and argue that the organization's activities should be discontinued or scaled back. This is in addition to critics who question UNRWA's existence because they believe it perpetuates Palestinian dependency and resentment against Israel.[70] However, many others, U.S. and Israeli officials included, assert that UNRWA plays a valuable role by providing stability and serving as the eyes and ears of the international community in Gaza. They generally characterize UNRWA's continued presence as preferable to the uncertain alternative that might emerge if UNRWA were removed from the picture,[71] presumably at least partly because Hamas or other groups appear incapable of

---

[69] CRS email correspondence with UNRWA official, September 23, 2013. As mentioned in footnote 65, aggregate contributions from the Muslim world constituted approximately 9% of UNRWA's total 2012 budget.

[70] See, e.g., Michael S. Bernstam, "The Palestinian Proletariat," *Commentary*, December 2010.

[71] See FY2015 Congressional Budget Justification for Foreign Operations, Department of State (Appendix 2), p. 134: "U.S. support for UNRWA directly contributes to the U.S. strategic interest of meeting the humanitarian needs of (continued...)

adequately addressing the needs of the refugees who comprise approximately two-thirds of Gaza's population.

Syria's ongoing conflict has significantly affected the more than 500,000 Palestinian refugees that were based there at the outset of the conflict in 2011. UNRWA has sought and continues to seek emergency funding to address these refugees' needs. According to the "Syria Crisis" portal on UNRWA's website as of July 3, 2014, 63% of these refugees have been displaced either within Syria or to neighboring countries.[72] Some Palestinian refugees in Syria have been killed or injured, and some have reportedly taken part in the conflict. Much international attention has focused on the ongoing plight of Palestinian refugees in Yarmouk camp, which is located in greater Damascus.[73] Future events could exacerbate or mitigate the dilemma of Palestinian refugees in Syria, with potential implications for UNRWA needs assessments.

Issues for Congress

Israeli officials and other observers periodically criticize UNRWA for various reasons. For example, some characterize the organization's vetting procedures as insufficient or flawed,[74] and some claim that it engages in "one-sided political advocacy."[75] UNRWA's website states that its role encompasses "global advocacy for Palestine refugees" in addition to the provision of assistance and protection. UNRWA's officials maintain that it fulfills its mandate as well as can be expected under challenging circumstances (i.e., UNRWA's lack of a robust policing capability and other operational limitations, political pressures, and security concerns).[76]

(...continued)

Palestinians, while promoting their self-sufficiency. UNRWA plays a stabilizing role in the Middle East through its assistance programs, serving as an important counterweight to extremist elements. Given UNRWA's unique humanitarian role in areas where terrorist organizations are active, the Department of State continues to monitor closely UNRWA's obligations to take all possible measures to keep terrorists from benefitting from U.S. government funding." See also Baruch Spiegel, "Jerusalem's Surprisingly Good Relations with UNRWA," *Middle East Quarterly*, vol. XIX, no. 4 (Fall 2012), pp. 61-66.

[72] UNRWA's "Syria Crisis" portal asserts that 270,000 refugees have been displaced within Syria, and reports that 53,070 have registered with UNRWA in Lebanon and 13,836 have done so in Jordan, with others having fled to Egypt, Libya, Gaza, Turkey, Malaysia, Thailand, and Indonesia. Jordan reportedly generally refuses entry by Palestinian refugees from Syria, or, in some cases, forcibly returns them. Jordan reportedly applies similar general policies to single men and undocumented individuals seeking to enter its territory from Syria.

[73] See, e.g., Nidal Bitari, "Yarmuk Refugee Camp and the Syrian Uprising: A View from Within," *Journal of Palestine Studies*, vol. XLIII, no. 1 (Autumn 2013), pp. 61-78; Salim Salamah, "Starving the Palestinian Yarmouk Camp," Carnegie Endowment for International Peace, April 28, 2014.

[74] James G. Lindsay (former general counsel for UNRWA), *Fixing UNRWA: Repairing the UN's Troubled System of Aid to Palestinian Refugees*, Washington Institute of Near East Policy, Policy Focus #91, January 2009; James Phillips, "The Gaza Aid Package: Time to Rethink U.S. Foreign Assistance to the Palestinians," The Heritage Foundation WebMemo No. 2333, March 9, 2009.

[75] Ibid. Israel Ministry of Foreign Affairs Statement: "Israel calls on UNRWA to refrain from one-sided political advocacy," August 27, 2013.

[76] A direct written rebuttal by Israeli academic Maya Rosenfeld to the former UNRWA general counsel's 2009 article was carried by UNRWA's website and is currently available at http://rete-eco.it/attachments/ 5172_Rejoinder%20to%20Lindsay_jan09.pdf.

Vetting of UNRWA Contributions

The primary concern raised by some Members of Congress is that U.S. contributions to UNRWA might be used to support terrorists. Section 301(c) of the 1961 Foreign Assistance Act (P.L. 87-195), as amended, says that "No contributions by the United States shall be made to [UNRWA] except on the condition that [UNRWA] take[s] all possible measures to assure that no part of the United States contribution shall be used to furnish assistance to any refugee who is receiving military training as a member of the so-called Palestine Liberation Army or any other guerrilla type organization or who has engaged in any act of terrorism."

A May 2009 GAO report said that, since a previous GAO report in 2003, UNRWA and the State Department had strengthened their policies and procedures to conform with Section 301(c) legal requirements, but that "weaknesses remain."[77] Neither report found UNRWA to be in noncompliance with Section 301(c), and to date, no arm of the U.S. government has made such a finding. The following are some points from the 2009 report and subsequent developments related to it:

- In the 2009 GAO report, State officials said compliance is evaluated based on State's "internal level of confidence that UNRWA has taken all possible measures to ensure that terrorists are not receiving assistance, such as having procedures in place and taking measures to respond to issues that arise."[78] State has not defined the term "all possible measures," nor has it defined what would constitute noncompliance with Section 301(c).

- The report said that State had not established written criteria to use in evaluating UNRWA's compliance with Section 301(c), and recommended that State consider doing so.[79] In November 2009, State and UNRWA signed a nonbinding "Framework for Cooperation" for 2010. The document agreed that, along with the compliance reports UNRWA submits to State biannually, State would use 15 enumerated criteria "as a way to evaluate" UNRWA's compliance with Section 301(c). State has signed a similar document with UNRWA in each subsequent year.[80]

- UNRWA said that it screens its staff and contractors every six months and that it screened all Palestinian refugees and microfinance clients in December 2008 for terrorist ties to Al Qaeda and the Taliban, pursuant to a list established pursuant to U.N. Security Council Resolution 1267.[81] According to the State Department, UNRWA has subsequently screened all of the above groups roughly every six months.[82] UNRWA said that it is unable to screen those of its beneficiaries who

---

[77] GAO, *Measures to Prevent Inadvertent Payments to Terrorists...*, op. cit.

[78] Ibid.

[79] Ibid.

[80] "Framework for Cooperation Between UNRWA and the Government of the United States of America for 2014," available at http://www.state.gov/documents/organization/218288.pdf. The 15 enumerated criteria are found in Annex 1 of the framework document.

[81] GAO, *Measures to Prevent Inadvertent Payments to Terrorists...*, op. cit.

[82] CRS correspondence with State Department official, June 20, 2012.

are displaced persons from the 1967 war because it does not collect information on those persons.[83]

- UNRWA's UN 1267 terrorist screening list does not include Hamas, Hezbollah, or most other militant groups that operate in UNRWA's surroundings. UNRWA is unwilling to screen its contractors and funding recipients against a list supplied by only one U.N. member state. Nevertheless, UNRWA officials did say that if notified by U.S. officials of potential matches, they would "use the information as a trigger to conduct their own investigation," which led to the report's recommendation that the State Department consider screening UNRWA contractors.[84] In response, State says that it now screens quarterly, against the Excluded Parties Lists System (EPLS, which is a list of parties excluded throughout the U.S. government from receiving federal contracts),[85]

  > the names of vendors of contracts equal to or exceeding $100,000, as provided by UNRWA. Each contract awardee is screened twice by separate State/PRM staff.... Since the EPLS screening by State/PRM began in 2009, the analysis has resulted in no matches against the EPLS.[86]

- UNRWA has established procedures to investigate inappropriate staff behavior. UNRWA said that it seeks information from authorities whenever staff are detained, convicted, or refused a permit or targeted by Israeli military forces. UNRWA officials said (in the 2009 GAO report) that they share the names of all UNRWA staff annually with the governments of Egypt, Israel, Jordan, Lebanon, Syria, and the Palestinian Authority.[87] In September 2013, UNRWA said that in the "few limited instances information about staff members from a government has been shared with UNRWA, it has been fully investigated and appropriate action has been taken."[88]

---

[83] GAO, *Measures to Prevent Inadvertent Payments to Terrorists...*, op. cit. In 2006, an organization that advocates for Palestinian refugees estimated the total number of 1967 displaced persons to be between 800,000 and 850,000. See BADIL Resource Center for Palestinian Residency & Refugee Rights, *Survey of Palestinian Refugees and Internally Displaced Persons 2004-2005*, May 2006.

[84] GAO, *Measures to Prevent Inadvertent Payments to Terrorists...*, op. cit.

[85] U.S. General Services Administration website at https://www.acquisition.gov/faqs_whatis.asp.

[86] CRS email correspondence with State Department official, December 4, 2012.

[87] GAO, *Measures to Prevent Inadvertent Payments to Terrorists...*, op. cit.

[88] CRS email correspondence with UNRWA official, September 23, 2013.

- UNRWA officials said that UNRWA provides assistance "in the context of its humanitarian mandate, meaning that agency policy is generally not to deny education or primary healthcare benefits." The officials said that if a refugee was denied benefits because of suspected militant or terrorist activities or ties, his or her child "would not be disqualified from attending an UNRWA school."[89]

Legislation and Oversight

Critiques of UNRWA's operations are routinely raised, and some Members of Congress have supported legislation or resolutions aimed at increasing oversight of the agency, strengthening its vetting procedures, and/or capping U.S. contributions.[90]

Some observers assert that UNRWA, by providing services to descendants of the original Palestinian refugees from 1948—by one count, the number of registered refugees has increased seven-fold since then—has effectively become "a silent partner to the Palestinian leadership" in perpetuating the refugee issue.[91] UNRWA officials insist—despite some observers' assertions to the contrary[92]— that established "principles and practice—as well as realities on the ground— clearly refute the argument that the right of return of Palestine refugees would disappear or be abandoned if UNHCR [the U.N. High Commissioner for Refugees, instead of UNRWA] were responsible for these refugees."[93] In September 2013 correspondence with CRS on this issue, a State Department official stated:

> In protracted refugee situations, refugee groups experience natural population growth over time. UNHCR and UNRWA both generally recognize descendants of refugees as refugees for purposes of their operations; this approach is not unique to the Palestinian context. For example, UNHCR recognizes descendants of refugees as refugees in populations including, but not limited to, the Burmese refugee population in Thailand, the Bhutanese refugee population in Nepal, the Afghan population in Pakistan, and the Somali population seeking refuge in neighboring countries.
>
> The United States' acceptance of UNRWA's method of recognizing refugees is unrelated to the final status issue of Palestinian refugees, which is to be resolved in negotiations between the parties.

Opposing views on this subject highlight a broader debate over responsibility for the multi-generational Israeli-Palestinian conflict and whether attempts to resolve the refugee problem

---

[89] Ibid.

[90] H.R. 3155 (United Nations Transparency, Accountability, and Reform Act of 2013) would require that any contribution made to UNRWA be subject to recent certification by the Secretary of State that UNRWA is complying with various self-policing and transparency-promoting activities, including measures UNRWA takes to prevent assistance to terrorists, and measures it takes to promote tolerance and employees' impartiality. Past legislative proposals and report language have contained similar certification or reporting requirements.

[91] Jonathan Schanzer, "Status Update," *foreignpolicy.com*, May 21, 2012.

[92] Josh Rogin, "Senate fight today over Palestinian 'refugees,'" *thecable.foreignpolicy.com*, May 24, 2012: "UNRWA has been using a definition that includes descendants of refugees while other U.N. bodies do not include descendants in their definition." See also Jennifer Rubin, "Is the U.N. making the Palestinian refugee problem worse?," *washingtonpost.com*, May 23, 2012.

[93] "Exploding the myths: UNRWA, UNHCR and Palestine refugees" (quoting UNRWA spokesman Chris Gunness), *maannews.net*, June 27, 2011. The article quotes Gunness as saying that "in all cases, refugees and their descendants retain the status of refugees until that status lapses through the achievement of a just and lasting solution."

separately are advisable and more likely either to lead to or work against an overall resolution that addresses both parties' interests.[94] In 2012, the Senate Appropriations Subcommittee on State, Foreign Operations, and Related Programs approved a reporting requirement in connection with FY2013 appropriations that, if enacted, would have required the Secretary of State to differentiate between the original 1948 refugees and their descendants. In a letter to the subcommittee, the State Department objected, asserting that this requirement would be "viewed around the world as the United States acting to prejudge and determine the outcome of this sensitive issue."[95]

Conclusion

Implementing U.S. bilateral assistance programs for the West Bank and Gaza and making UNRWA contributions routinely present challenges due to regional political uncertainty, ongoing Israeli-Palestinian disputes, concerns over the composition and behavior of the PA government, and concerns that aid might be diverted to Palestinian terrorist groups. Nevertheless, the PA remains dependent on external donor assistance to meet its budgetary needs—especially its large public payroll—and it also seeks foreign investment to jumpstart its private sector.

In assessing whether U.S. aid to the Palestinians has advanced U.S. interests in recent years, Congress could evaluate how successful aid has been in

- reducing the threat of terrorism;

- inclining Palestinians towards peace with Israel;

- preparing Palestinians for self-reliance in security, political, and economic matters;

- promoting regional stability; and

- meeting humanitarian needs.

Even if the immediate objectives of U.S. assistance programs for the Palestinians are met, the long-term utility of U.S. aid in encouraging regional stability and Palestinian economic and political self-sufficiency might depend to some extent on progress toward a political solution that addresses Palestinian national aspirations and Israeli security demands.

Congress's assessment of the effectiveness of past aid in the context of U.S. policy priorities might influence its deliberations over

- which aid programs to start, continue, expand, scale back, change, or end; and

- which oversight, vetting, monitoring, and evaluation requirements to apply to various aid programs.

---

[94] See, e.g., Hilary Leila Krieger, "Palestinians: US refugee bill may delay peace," *jpost.com*, June 5, 2012; Leila Hilal, "Israeli Leader Wrongly Blames UN and Arab States for Palestinian Refugees," *theatlantic.com*, February 21, 2012; "Leila Hilal's bizarre defense of UNRWA," *jpost.com* (Warped Mirror Blog), June 7, 2012.

[95] Text of letter dated May 24, 2012, from Deputy Secretary of State Thomas Nides to Senator Patrick Leahy, Chairman of the Senate Appropriations Subcommittee on State, Foreign Operations, and Related Programs available at http://www.scribd.com/doc/94703915/DepSec-State-Opposes-Kirk-Amdt#download.

Appendix A. Congressional Holds on FY2011 and FY2012 Aid

Various Members of congressional committees with jurisdiction over the authorization and appropriation of U.S. aid to the Palestinians placed informal holds on the obligation of various portions of already-appropriated FY2011 and FY2012 assistance for the Palestinians. This was apparently largely because of Palestinian initiatives within the U.N. system seeking greater international recognition of Palestinian statehood.

Congressional holds on foreign aid are not legally binding on the executive branch. However, since the late 1970s/early 1980s, successive Administrations have generally deferred to holds placed by Members of pertinent committees. This is part of a process by which the executive branch consults with Congress to provide it with information or otherwise address committees' concerns prior to obligating funds subject to a hold. In 2007 and 2008, Representative Nita Lowey, then chairwoman of the House Appropriations Subcommittee on State, Foreign Operations, and Related Programs, exercised holds partly in order to shape the conditions under which the United States could provide budgetary and security assistance to the West Bank-based PA following Hamas's takeover of Gaza and its dismissal from the PA government.[96]

By March 2012, all Members other than then House Foreign Affairs Committee Chairman Ileana Ros-Lehtinen had reportedly decided to release their holds on FY2011 funds.[97] In April 2012, the *National Journal* reported that Secretary of State Hillary Clinton had decided to provide the entire remaining amount of appropriated FY2011 ESF project assistance despite Chairman Ros-Lehtinen's hold.[98] The report cited an unnamed State Department official as stating that the funds deliver

> critical support to the Palestinian people and those leaders seeking to combat extremism within their society and build a more stable future. Without funding, our programs risk cancellation. Such an occurrence would undermine the progress that has been made in recent years in building Palestinian institutions and improving stability, security, and economic prospects, which benefits Israelis and Palestinians alike.[99]

Prior to the release of congressional holds on FY2012 funding, the U.S. Agency for International Development (USAID) provided the following information to CRS on January 17, 2013:

> Due to the existing hold on FY 2012 [economic support] funding, six projects were expected to close between March and May 2013. USAID therefore instructed the Chief of Parties for these projects to decelerate their project activities to continue a lower level of project implementation—in other words, to extend the duration of the program. With this deceleration, the six projects are now expected to have sufficient funding through dates that

---

[96] "Splits Between U.S. and Europe Over Aid to Palestinians," *International Herald Tribune*, February 22, 2007; "Appropriator Wants Palestinian Authority Aid on Hold Until Accountability in Place," *CQ Today*, March 4, 2008.

[97] "U.S. lawmakers release $88.6 million in aid to Palestinians," *Reuters*, April 4, 2012. According, to this article, Ros-Lehtinen reportedly agreed to release her hold over all but approximately $60 million of the Economic Support Fund project assistance for the West Bank and Gaza, subject to various conditions.

[98] Sara Sorcher, "Clinton Overrules Republican Lawmaker's Hold on Palestinian Aid," *nationaljournal.com*, April 11, 2012.

[99] Ibid.

---

vary by project, between May-September 2013. All other USAID-funded projects are expected to run out of existing funds between June-December 2013 if they maintain a normal project implementation rate. Deceleration can involve the downsize of the project presence in country, including the termination of implementing partner staff.

On Dec. 30, 2012, the first termination notices were sent out to 17 partner staff working on the Health Flagship program implemented by Chemonics. The remaining 40 termination notices are expected to go out to the Health Flagship implementing partner staff between January 28, 2013 and March 31, 2013.

Appendix B. The Role of Arab States

Members of Congress have indicated an interest in staying abreast of the economic assistance that Arab state governments provide to the West Bank and the PA, sometimes requiring reports from the Administration on the subject.[100] Arab states (especially Gulf states) provided large amounts of aid to the Hamas-led PA government in 2006-2007 after the United States and European Union withdrew their aid, but following the reinstitution of U.S. and EU aid in mid-2007, most of them reduced contributions.[101] Routinely, they make generous pledges of aid to the Palestinians, but at times fulfill them only in part and after significant delay. The largest Arab donor to the PA budget is Saudi Arabia, which generally contributes between $100 million-$260 million annually (see **Figure 1**).

Arab governments' reluctance to fulfill pledges may stem from misgivings over "picking sides" in Palestinian factional disputes and from concerns that without imminent prospects either for domestic political unity or for progress on the peace process, any money contributed could be a waste. On the part of the Gulf states in particular, reluctance may also stem from a feeling that they are less responsible historically for the Palestinians' current situation than Israel, the United States, and Europe.[102] Also, according to *Reuters*, "A high of $1.8 billion in foreign aid [from Arab countries for the benefit of the West Bank-based PA] in 2008 plunged to $600 million [in 2012], with Gulf countries scaling back their giving because of increased domestic spending over two years of Arab political uprisings and the global financial downturn."[103]

Author Contact Information

Jim Zanotti
Specialist in Middle Eastern Affairs
jzanotti@crs.loc.gov, 7-1441

---

[100] See, e.g., H.Rept. 111-366 (to P.L. 111-117, Consolidated Appropriations Act, 2010): "The conferees direct the Secretary of State to provide a report to the Committees on Appropriations not later than 180 days after enactment of this Act on international participation, including by Arab states, in the economic development of the West Bank and support for the Palestinian Authority, similar to that proposed by the House. This report may be submitted in classified form, if necessary."

[101] See Glenn Kessler, "Arab Aid to Palestinians Often Doesn't Fulfill Pledges," *Washington Post*, July 27, 2008; "Falling Short," *Washington Post*, July 27, 2008.

[102] See, e.g., Robert Bowker, *Palestinian Refugees: Mythology, Identity, and the Search for Peace*, Boulder, CO: Lynn Rienner Publications, Inc., 2003, p. 194.

[103] "Saudis to give $100 million to Palestinian Authority," *Reuters*, January 16, 2013.